BRITAIN'S RAILWAYS IN TRANSITION 1965–75
All Change
John Evans

AMBERLEY

First published 2017

Amberley Publishing
The Hill, Stroud
Gloucestershire, GL5 4EP

www.amberley-books.com

Copyright © John Evans, 2017

The right of John Evans to be identified as the
Author of this work has been asserted in accordance
with the Copyrights, Designs and Patents Act 1988.

ISBN 978 1 4456 6386 9 (print)
ISBN 978 1 4456 6387 6 (ebook)

British Library Cataloguing in Publication Data.
A catalogue record for this book is available from
the British Library.

Typeset in 10pt on 13pt Celeste.
Typesetting by Amberley Publishing.
Printed in the UK.

Introduction

It is a day of hazy sunshine during late October 1965. I am standing on the platform at Northampton Castle station – a building in transition. Symbolically, the north end of the station dates back to London and North Western Railway days. The southern end has been rebuilt with modern canopies. In the bay platform is a diesel multiple unit, recently arrived from Rugby. A train is signalled from the north and an English Electric Type 4 passes through hauling a long rake of empty wagons. Minutes later and another freight, comprising modern wagons built to carry Ford cars, rumbles past headed by a blue electric locomotive: No. E3165. I wait nearly half an hour for the next movement – it is a Stanier 8F, also heading north on freight, but this time making for the Market Harborough line. Steam, diesel and electric power, all working together.

British Railways was in transition. Despite a deep affection for steam inside me, I had to admit that the railway scene at this confusing time was totally fascinating. Using my detailed notes, many friends on the website Flickr, old books and magazines, and fading memories, I have compiled some highlights of those years which support the illustrations.

It is in 1965 that this book starts – a year when I picked up my first roll of colour film and started using my new single lens reflex camera, bought with a loan from my dad. There was so much to record, so little time to do it: a ride on the Bournemouth Belle Pullman train; visits to the north that could at last be afforded; recording the last vestiges of steam and the last rites of old branch lines; a trip along the whole of the Great Central; seeing the last of steam in Wales; celebrating the advent of the new railway that seemed so long coming; and watching the high speed network of the future take shape.

This book buys you a seat next to me on my travels. By starting work, I could at last afford to run a car and purchase colour film. My trusty friends Bryan Jeyes and Bob Mullins, whose pictures help to improve this book, joined in the fun for the first few years until we went our separate ways in search of employment. When I put down my camera in nostalgic exasperation in 1969 and 1970, I left a gap that has very kindly been filled by photographers who were made of sterner stuff – Gordon Edgar and Terry Campbell. I took two pictures in 1970 and 200 in 1972!

I hope you enjoy looking at the pictures and the stories they tell. I am obliged to John Simmonds for identifying some of the trains from their head codes and I am also very grateful to the team at Amberley for making these pictures come to life after lying dormant in slide boxes for forty years and more.

John Evans
Luddenden, West Yorkshire, 2016

The Wilderness Years

British Railways ran the last main-line passenger train hauled by a steam locomotive on 11 August 1968. Crowds lined the tracks as a small group of specially prepared locomotives conveyed a privileged group of travellers from Liverpool to Carlisle and back. It marked the conclusion of 150 years of valiant service from one of the great inventions of the modern age; a machine which mobilised and liberated the nation and later the world. For the many who had followed steam's increasingly rushed annihilation since the Modernisation Plan of 1955, a new era had begun. Things would never be quite the same again. It was Bob Dylan picking up an electric guitar at Manchester Free Trade Hall; the first time you made a mobile phone call; Karl Benz driving down a street in Mannheim in the world's first car.

After the frantic summer of 1968, a period of three wilderness years commenced. Platform ends seemed bereft of enthusiasts. The railway press was short of real stories. There were various schemes in their infancy to preserve actual railways, spurred on by the success of the Bluebell, the Dart Valley and Keighley and Worth Valley lines, the last of which re-opened that summer. Others, including the Severn Valley Railway, were making progress towards gaining a Light Railway Order, but it would be well into the 1970s before the network of heritage railways that we have today started to take shape.

At some time during late 1964, the number of diesel and electric locomotives in service with British Railways exceeded the number of steam engines. It's hard to pin down an exact date, as steam engines were being withdrawn daily and new traction was entering service with similar regularity. To get a better picture of what was happening we must include the vast fleet of multiple unit trains swamping both main and secondary lines. One thing we can be sure about – 1964 was the last year when steam seemed the dominant machine on locomotive-hauled trains. From the end of that year it was on a downward spiral, like a crippled aircraft making its final plunge to its inevitable doom.

During May 1964 I paid a visit to Crewe Works and was amazed at the huge number of Brush Type 4 diesels (later Class 47) being built. The production line resembled that of a car factory, with rows of locomotives in various stages of construction. It was the Brush Type 4 that changed everything. Here was a locomotive being built in large quantities (more than 500 were eventually delivered) and seemingly able to tackle any task thrown at it. The fact that some of them are still at work fifty years later is testament to the sound design and, like a boxer just toying with his opponent before delivering the knock-out punch, the Class 47 would floor the remaining main-line steam engines in four years. Even so, the early days of these engines were beset by issues. They were aided by a variety of other products, especially the English Electric Type 3 (Class 37), a medium-weight slogger, and more than a thousand 0-6-0 shunters of basically 1940s design, which dispatched an army of steam shunters to the grave. No respecter of youth, these types also managed to cause extra devastation with some 'friendly fire.' Not only was steam seen off by 1968, but some of those early diesels went too. British Rail – flaunting its proud new blue image and double-arrow symbol – lost patience with several of its pioneering designs and shortly after eliminating steam decided that some of those unsatisfactory diesels should join their forebears. At least the steam engines were reliable; what could you do with a Baby Deltic that had been built and rebuilt within ten years and was still hopeless, or a smoky old two-stroke Metrovick Co-Bo that looked as bad as it performed? Many of these early diesels had been built as part of the 1955 Modernisation Plan, which created orders for small batches of engines from manufacturers who often had little experience building diesels. The plan was to launch an area by area conversion to modern traction, but really this only happened in East Anglia. After that, there was a headstrong rush to introduce diesel locomotives and multiple units without much strategic thinking.

Muddled Thinking

The British Transport Commission had drawn up ambitious plans covering not just the introduction of new locomotives, but extensive improvements to the railway infrastructure as well. It's difficult to assess exactly how much money was spent, but most observers consider it to be somewhere north of £1.6 billion (about £40 billion in today's money). It was envisaged that the best steam locomotives would work on into the 1970s and that, for many lines, diesels would be a stopgap until electrification. But this was a time of sweeping change, with hungry road haulage companies and bus operators eating into the railways' traditional markets. A new competitor, then in its infancy, was air travel, which was soon offering a network of intercity flights that enticed the long-distance rail passenger.

The orders for new traction, placed at a time when the last steam shunters had not been delivered and a programme to rebuild 140 Southern Pacifics had just been launched, suggested that around 2,500 diesels would be needed, plus a big fleet of diesel multiple units. Many of the companies that received orders for diesel locomotives had little or no experience of building modern traction. The North British

Locomotive Company – a famed builder of fine steam power – built 160 useless diesels for British Railways and the enormous warranty costs helped to send them to the wall. All these early orders, from five to twenty engines, were known as the 'pilot scheme' and it was intended to gain experience with them before committing to large orders. In the event, this didn't really happen and a large number of extra orders was placed before the prototypes had been evaluated. The operating department soon found itself floundering with certain problematic types.

There was also a major issue about training. Steam crews of varying ability had to be quickly trained to work the new machines and an army of maintenance teams, supported by the manufacturers, was needed to keep the new locomotives going. A friend of mine was a steam driver at the time and took three attempts to pass out on diesels. It was quite simply a radical new world, shifting from the simple to the complex and from a machine that could often be coaxed home if suffering maladies to a recalcitrant diesel no amount of crew skill could get back to base. Among the worst were the Co-Bo Metrovicks, which were handed back to the manufacturers as a class for modification, and the Baby Deltics, which at one time were all in store out of use. While we think of the Brush Type 2 as a successful and long-lived machine, remember that the whole class was fitted with new English Electric engines within a few years of construction as the original Mirrlees units suffered fractures.

Probably the most experienced builder was English Electric, which had provided mechanical parts for many diesel shunters and the five main-line diesels then at work (10000/10001 and 10201–10203). There was also a smaller 800 bhp North British diesel, No. 10800, in service. The first engine to be delivered under the Modernisation Plan was English Electric Type 1 No. D8000 in 1957, one of the new types that proved to be an enduring success as several of them are still at work today.

There were five main power categories for the new diesels, organised in engine power:

Type 1	800–1,000 bhp	D8000–D8616, D9500–D9555
Type 2	1,001–1,499 bhp	D5000–D6357, D7500–D7677
Type 3	1,500–1,999 bhp	D6500–D7100
Type 4	2,000–2,999 bhp	D1–D1999
Type 5	Above 3,000 bhp	D9000–D9021

Obviously the arrival of such a vast fleet of new engines played havoc with the existing army of steam locomotives. Ten years after the launch of the Modernisation Plan, when I first filled my new Petriflex single lens reflex camera with a roll of colour film, the death of steam was entering its final phase. For the enthusiast, this was in some ways the most interesting period of our railways in transition. You could see express trains hauled by A4 Pacifics in Scotland or Bulleid Pacifics on the Southern; blue electrics were taking over on the West Coast Main Line, but there was plenty of steam still in service, and the variety of diesels everywhere was enormous. The chart below shows how that transition took place, with the number of different locomotives in service (excluding multiple units) shrinking from 150 to thirty-five in just ten years.

(For the purposes of this survey, derivative types, such as Classes 44, 45 and 46 are counted as one, as are Classes 26/27, 24/25 etc.)

Locomotives in service by number of classes

	1965	1968	1971	1975
Steam	92	8	o	o
Diesels				
Type 5:	1	1	1	1
Type 4:	7	7	8	6
Type 3:	4*	3	3	3
Type 2:	7	7	6	3
Type 1:	5	5	2	1
Shunters:	26	18	14	9
Electric□:	12	13	10	12
Total:	154	62	44	35

(plus departmental locomotives)

* Includes LMS No. 10001
□ Includes electro-diesels

Withdrawal of the early pilot diesels started in 1967. A new *National Traction Plan* was created, aimed at reducing the number of diesel classes in service from twenty-eight to fifteen by 1974 through elimination of unreliable and non-standard types. This included all the diesel hydraulic engines, of which more than 300 were at work in 1967. At the end of that year the five non-standard Warship locomotives Nos D600–D604 were taken out of service and the Metrovick Co-Bo engines, with their crude two stroke power units, soon followed. I was amazed to visit a Kettering steam scrapyard in 1969 to find two Baby Deltic diesels among the industrial steam engines awaiting cutting up. It was like seeing two generations of technology suffering oblivion on the same day.

This book is arranged sequentially, opening in 1965 when I started work in Northampton. Every photograph was precious and expensive, as a role of 35 mm colour transparency film with processing cost a third of a week's wages. Many of those early pictures were taken in Northampton, where I lived at the time, but by the end of the period under review I was travelling throughout the country. These excursions entailed several memorable trips, including a long journey on the Thames-Clyde Express from Kettering to Carlisle behind three different Peak Class diesels. From comments made to me by colleagues, I seem to have returned to photography following the demise of steam much quicker than many other enthusiasts. Somewhere around the middle of the period covered by this book, the 'G' word raised its head (Girls!) and caused a few blips in my railway activities. The trick, of course, was to find a girl who didn't mind standing on a damp platform watching a blue and yellow engine flash past and being told 'not to stand there because you'll be in the picture', or one who was prepared to clamber aboard a smelly, bouncy Mark One coach and take a wintry trip over the Settle-Carlisle line, or who would join a visit to a nascent steam centre, which appeared to contain the decaying contents of a local breakers' yard. If she could tell the difference between a 9F and a Duchess Pacific, so much the better. Such women, I can assure you, do exist!

Decline and Fall

In the 1950s, a rail enthusiast living in my home town of Northampton could take a trip to Bedford, Euston, Blisworth, Daventry, Rugby, Market Harborough, Wellingborough, and Peterborough. Like many towns, we had two stations and a veritable spider's web of destinations in the immediate vicinity. By 1965, Dr Beeching (and BR itself) had started chipping away at them until, by 1975, there was just one station and one line, running north to south from Rugby to Euston. The 'replacement bus service,' so confidently proclaimed as the happy new transport artery, often withered and died without any real fuss. You could, for example, catch a bus today from Northampton to Peterborough, but it would take two hours twenty three minutes, or you could travel by train via London for fifty pounds! The old Northampton to Peterborough line was slow ... but not that slow. To Market Harborough takes about the same time with two changes. To be fair, these days you can get a bus from Northampton to Towcester, a ten-mile journey, which would have required a change of train and a lengthy wait at Blisworth in steam days. The sixty-five-mile journey from Northampton to London Euston currently takes around an hour and there is a frequent service, but surely the 11.37 a.m. from Northampton in 1962 could match that (although running non-stop, it has to be said)?

A Time of Turmoil

This journey starts in the middle of 1965 and ends ten years later. So much changed during that period, as complete main lines disappeared, the classic freight marshalling yards shrank in size and number, and Dr Beeching's scalpel was still in use, some lines taking longer to expunge than expected. Certainly the railway map and the method of operating changed in many ways. I once recall seeing a caption to a photograph of a branch line labelled 'A page not in Dr Beeching's book.' There are plenty of those within this volume.

In 1961 the railway industry in the UK employed more than 450,000 people. Dr Beeching's plan cut 67,000 jobs, 2,000 stations, and 4,000 miles from the route map. By 1981 there were still 360,000 railway employees (fewer than 80,000 now work for the railway industry). In my home county, the number of railway stations declined from about seventy to just six. Elsewhere, we would never have imagined that huge stations like Bournemouth West, Bradford Exchange, and Sheffield Victoria would totally disappear.

And yet somehow, against what must have been totally demotivating changes for many staff, the new blue railway struggled on. The double arrow symbol, mocked at first as suggesting British Rail didn't know whether it was coming or going, has survived a myriad of changes and is now the national identifier for a railway station. Though a time of turmoil, the 1965–75 period showed the way ahead for Britain's railways and some of the scenes depicted at the end of this book look very different from the old-style railway you will see in the 1965 photographs.

The book is organised into two sections – a diary of events for each year and then a section of photographs. These reflect many of the events mentioned in the diary section, but have been chosen more to portray the main line railways than the growing nucleus of heritage lines that sprung up in the early 1970s. A few interesting curios are also shown – such as the electric locomotive No. E2001 and some strange double-headers. Sometimes you just happened to be in the right place at the right time with your camera.

1965 – Into the Wide Blue Yonder

In 1965, British Railways changed its name and its corporate identity. From now on it would be British Rail and the familiar double-sausage station signs and lion-on-wheel emblem on rolling stock would be replaced by a double arrow. The previous year, a Class 47 diesel had been repainted in blue with a red panel, on which was displayed the new double arrow symbol. The coaches were painted blue and white and it actually looked pretty good. In the event, the red panel disappeared and resulted in the blue livery looking rather severe as there was no relief, save for the yellow ends. Steam locomotives, meanwhile, would not be treated to the new colours, except for the three Vale of Rheidol narrow gauge engines, still owned by British Rail.

Dr Richard Beeching, the BR Board chairman, firstly produced a report called *The Reshaping of British Railways* in 1963, followed by another in 1965 outlining which main lines should receive investment and which should not, entitled *The Development of the Major Railway Trunk Routes*. At a press conference, he stressed that it was not a prelude to further closures, but pessimistically pointed out the duplication of routes from London to Scotland and across the Pennines. This sounded worryingly like ... a prelude to further closures.

In 1965, 600 miles of railway closed, with the North East and East Anglia being hardest hit. In contrast, electrification of the West Coast Main Line was the major investment project for BR, the first trains running trials into Euston in November 1965. The frequent sight of electrification engineering trains, usually hauled by steam locomotives, was a poignant reminder that things were about to change forever. The condemned man was being forced to carry the hanging rope.

As far as locomotives were concerned, the relentless assault on the remaining steam engines continued. It was the last year when you could find steam at work on the Western Region, so all the remaining Great Western engines were withdrawn, with the exception of a few mainly smaller types that operated in areas that had moved to the London Midland. It was also the last year when British Railways owned completely intact classes of steam locomotives – the Standard Britannia Pacifics and Class 3 2-6-0s suffered their first withdrawals in 1965. Classes of distinction that disappeared that year included the Great Western Castles and Halls, the LNER A3 Pacifics, and the venerable Great Central O4 2-8-0s. Other notable events during the year included the withdrawal of *Evening Star*.

The most significant new type introduced was probably the Class AL6 3500 bhp electric engine, later Class 86. Among locomotives in production were the Class 14 diesel-hydraulic 0-6-0s at Swindon, withdrawals of which started only three years later. Production of another very short-lived class, the unreliable Clayton Type 1 Bo-Bo, was also completed.

Looking back through the photographs I took that year brings back many memories. One problem concerned the wide choice of transparency film – there was Kodachrome II, Ektachrome, Perutz, Ferraniacolour, Ilford, and Agfa. Over a couple of years I tried them all, occasionally switching back to black and white prints when funds ran short.

There were some memorable trips that year. We purchased our usual 'Runabout' ticket in the summer, giving travel all over the East Midlands. Bryan Jeyes, my regular partner on rail trips, and I also made the heady purchase of a ticket on the Bournemouth Belle from our local travel agent. We were rewarded with a spotless Merchant Navy Pacific on the down trip, and while a brief visit to the beach was mandatory, we were soon back at Bournemouth West to watch some real action. We also became more interested in railway history and started walking some of our closed local lines, either before they were lifted, or shortly after.

The Great Central clung to life, as did the Derby to Manchester route. But our local shed, Northampton, finally shut its doors in September 1965 and our way of life changed. It was quite odd – no rushing down to the engine shed for half an hour before homework. The local ironstone railway scene changed too; there were more closures and a feeling that not just our local railway network, but also the deeply gouged countryside, with its scars from endless quarrying, would never be quite the same.

Sadly we were denied some of the more intriguing outposts of the rail network that year. A trip to see the last A4 Pacifics in Scotland was financially impossible. The North East, still with plenty of steam, was also too far; besides, we had many old friends to bid farewell to – the motley collection of LMS types that were at last yielding to modern traction on our local lines. And if all else failed there were still the new diesels, some of which were due for a very short life in the limelight. The English Electric Class 40s, for example, were already being superseded by bright blue electric engines and the Type 2 Class 24s were about to be moved aside in favour of AM10 four-car electric units.

Plus ça change...

1966 – The Noose Tightens

A particularly depressing year for Britain's railways, 1966 saw the closure of the Great Central main line. Even though it was a shadow of its former self, with vast stations welcoming infrequent trains, it had a very special character of its own. It closed in September with the last express an excursion hauled by a Merchant Navy Pacific. We all went to Brackley station and stood there with other mourners to watch the train head south on a very pleasant September afternoon. As it sped across Brackley viaduct and into the distance we quietly left the platforms and went home. It was a very solemn occasion. The only surviving sections were from Aylesbury to Marylebone and an inconvenient local passenger service connecting Rugby Central and Nottingham Victoria.

Another much-loved through route, the Somerset and Dorset Railway closed in March after an attempt to shut it in January was postponed. It was my first and last visit to the line. All services on the Keswick–Cockermouth line were also withdrawn – how I would have loved to try that line! Meanwhile, to raise a bit of cash for BR, the very convenient Blackpool Central station was sold for redevelopment.

By contrast, the new blue electric services commenced on the West Coast Main Line in April, looking somewhat strange as they often hauled old maroon coaches.

A less well-known event was the completion by Beyer-Peacock of its last locomotives, some Class 25 diesels for the London Midland Region. In fact delivery of diesels continued apace, with production of the venerable English Electric Type 1 restarting and other types to be delivered included the last of 100 Class 86 electrics and the Class 73 electro-diesels. During the year, as steam retrenched, sheds in North Wales, on much of the Midland line, and in the North East closed. Only the Southern main line, the North West, Leeds Holbeck, and the North East retained steam in any numbers, and the hard-working 9Fs and WDs on Tyne Dock–Consett ore trains finally gave way to diesels. The Swanage branch was among many dieselised, but steam held out on the Cambrian main line for freight and the main expresses only, with a batch of Standard Class 4 2-6-0 and 4-6-0 engines kept busy. Casualties during the year included the last LMS 4F 0-6-0s, A4 Pacifics, the Royal Scot 4-6-0s, Great Western pannier tanks, the 5600 0-6-2Ts, the N and U 2-6-0s, and the Southern Q1; Oswestry, Southampton Terminus, and both Glasgow Buchanan Street and the magnificent St Enoch station also closed.

The Ian Allan *British Railways Steam Locomotives* book issued at the end of 1965 was a worryingly slim volume, and by the time we bought it in early 1966 many of the locomotives listed had already been withdrawn. Steam open days started to appear – a kind of prelude to the start of the heritage railway movement.

Locally, our major casualty was the Rugby Midland to Peterborough North line through Market Harborough and Seaton. It was a railway we used often, finding it a particularly useful link. The last day of services in June 1966 was an all-diesel event, even though we heard a Black 5 would be brought to Rugby for the occasion. As the steam shed at Rugby had been closed for more than a year at this time, it was a bit of a long shot, although Nuneaton, just a few miles north, was a steam shed until June 1966. During 1966, Bryan and I spent a week in Wales on a railway holiday and were blessed with sunny weather. Later in 1966 I went on what was to be my last rail tour for many years; the Eight Counties Rail Tour. This was a wonderful day out, starting and ending at Northampton and covering several lines that I had not traversed before. These included Northampton to Market Harborough, Nottingham northwards on the Great Central and across the Woodhead route (behind the very first EM1 electric, No. 26000 *Tommy*). Standing at Shirebrook North alongside an immaculate Class B1 4-6-0, I had no idea that this was to be her last run in service and No. 61302 was withdrawn after the trip. That was 1966 – a year of lasts.

Approaching 2,700 miles of railway had been lost since the Beeching Report was published in 1963. Also withdrawn from service in 1966 was British Rail's last horse!

1967 – A Southern Lament

Diesels were not invincible. BR started withdrawals of some of the less successful pilot scheme machines, including, at the end of the year, all five North British D600 Warships, the hapless Metrovick Co-Bo engines, and the unsatisfactory North British Type 2 diesel hydraulic and diesel electric fleet. During the year more than 250 diesel locomotives were withdrawn from service. Newcomers included the first English Electric Type 4 (Class 50) No. D400. Deliveries of Brush Type 4 (Class 47) diesels were nearing the end.

The Glasgow suburban electrification scheme was completed and most regions announced faster schedules for many trains. Changes included the closure of the Stour Valley line and the ending of through trains from Paddington to Birkenhead and the Cambrian line. Nottingham Victoria – terminus of the surviving Great Central service from Rugby Central – closed, to be replaced by the previously shut Arkwright Street station. Ominously, the London Midland Region were making noises about axing that service as well.

Steam ended on the Southern Region on 5 July followed by some last day specials hauled by Merchant Navy Pacifics Nos 35028 *Clan Line* and 35008 *Orient Line*. There was then a big movement of redundant Southern steam westwards, with many engines gathered at Salisbury before making their final journeys to scrapyards. We made the pilgrimage, along with lots of other people, to see the last of Southern steam. At Hook we watched steam at express speed, yanked up the shutter speed on our cameras, and were rewarded with some good shots. To see expresses flying by at top speed with steam was a real treat.

The Isle of Wight also switched to modern power – in this case veteran London Transport tube trains – in March. A minor, but historically important, purchase involved 2-6-2T No. 41241 by the Keighley and Worth Valley Railway and it has been a mainstay of the line ever since. Another significant acquisition was A4 No. 60009 *Union of South Africa* by John Cameron, the start of a fifty-year relationship. A batch of Southern Region electric locomotives of the E5000 design was sent to Crewe for rebuilding as electro-diesels, although these turned out to be unsuccessful due to problems and, eventually, a lack of work. I was very surprised to see one of them at Crewe South shed in February 1967, before I realised what was happening.

Bryan and I made a great trip to see steam on the London Midland Region early in the year and hardly saw any diesels or electrics when visiting Crewe South and Chester sheds. It was also the year when one of our favourite lines – the Cromford and High Peak – closed. Leeds City station was rebuilt and re-opened to serve all train services. Despite the increasingly 'make-do-and-mend' approach to keeping steam locomotives running, there were still many diesel failures with clapped out Class 5s often called to the rescue. This was also the last year of the Britannias in normal service and they were kept busy on many extras, specials, freights and parcels work. A visit to Shap in 1967 would still produce a reasonable array of steam power, which was gradually confined to the North West. All non-standard diesel shunters were starting to be withdrawn.

Flicking through old magazines of the period reveals an amazing number of preservation appeals; some of these succeeded, while others sadly fell by the wayside. The failures included a J37 0-6-0, a Crab, a Stanier 2-6-4 tank, a Crosti 9F and a B1 (although another was saved). Classes rendered extinct included, of course, the Bulleid Pacifics, the North Eastern Q6, the Jubilee 4-6-0s and the J27, J36, J37 and J38 0-6-0s, which went along with all other Scottish steam stock. Britannia Pacific No. 70013 became the last steam engine to be overhauled by BR at the beginning of 1967. The year saw the end of the B1s and also of the steam-hauled freights on iron ore trains from Bidston to Shotwick – a great favourite with enthusiasts. Bulleid Pacifics Nos 34023 and 35028 were purchased for preservation.

The closure of the Oxford–Bletchley service at the end of the year was particularly unpleasant. When the passengers arrived back at Bletchley, we stood around chatting on the platform for a few minutes before an unduly aggressive member of the station staff came and ordered everyone to leave the station. Hardly a fond farewell. The Bedford–Cambridge section of the same line closed on the same day. Now, of course, the plan is to re-open it. The Padstow branch, much loved by many enthusiasts, also succumbed.

A word of praise here for those organisations that saved carriages – our world today is richer for their efforts, as the clear-out of redundant BR rolling stock included a huge number of very old and precious coaches, a few of which have survived thanks to the efforts of far-sighted individuals.

Years of heroic banking duties at Shap also came to an end when the depot at Tebay closed to steam at the end of the year. Listen to Peter Handford's recordings on the album *Shap* to recapture these wonderful sounds.

1968 – Hello, Goodbye

The 1968 Transport Act saw the creation of five Passenger Transport Authorities (later PTEs) and introduced subsidies for socially necessary, but loss-making lines. At last we had a group of local people with an interest in actually promoting rail transport. The act also wrote off BR's accumulated debt. Yet still the finales continued, though the pace had slowed down considerably. Closures in Scotland saw the end of the unloved four-wheel diesel rail buses, one of which was used for a time on our local Northampton to Bedford branch (before being replaced by steam!). Other services to close included stopping trains between Derby and Manchester, Three Bridges to East Grinstead, Chester to Hawarden Bridge, Hailsham to Eastbourne, lines in the Dunfermline area, and the Alnwick branch.

The Ian Allan Combined Volume issued early in the year contained details of just eight standard gauge steam classes. Steam was by now confined mainly to the North West and parts of Yorkshire, with Black 5s still hauling a few passenger services. Carnforth, Lostock Hall, and Rose Grove were the final three steam sheds – a haven for enthusiasts. Somehow they kept the declining stock of Class 5s, 8Fs, 9Fs and Standards going. In August, after a crazy flurry of specials, it was all over. British Rail ran its final main-line steam train and 150 years of passion, inventiveness and hard work became historical memories. Among all this decline of steam, the Keighley and Worth Valley Railway re-opened.

During the year it was announced that 4-6-0 No. 6000 *King George V* was to go to Bulmers, the cider makers, for restoration. By November the '*King*' and five Pullman cars had been restored to working order. This turned out to be a momentous decision for the steam movement in this country, although it did not appear so at the time. It seemed an unlikely home for a major steam locomotive. I raise a glass to Bulmers every now and then for starting the Return to Steam movement.

In September 1968, Class 4F 0-6-0 No. 43924 became the first locomotive to leave Barry scrapyard, a procession that was to continue for another twenty years. She had been in the yard for less than three years, but some would wait more than twenty-four years for resurrection. One of the issues facing locomotive purchasers at the time (and also the curator of BR's relics) was where to house them. Today's network of heritage railways did not exist and finding a location for a large steam engine was a major headache; hence, of course, the Bulmers factor.

Movements of withdrawn Southern locomotives continued during 1968 and it would be the end of the year before the last engines

(I believe these were 35030 and 34017) were cut up. Just one LNER engine remained in capital stock – K1 No. 62005 – which clung to life as if pleading for rescue. It spent the early weeks of 1968 in use as a stationary boiler. Luckily that rescue came.

The *National Traction Plan* was published at the end of the year calling for unreliable and non-standard diesel locomotives to be withdrawn to reduce the many different types of diesels then at work. A start was made on eliminating the new but very unsatisfactory Clayton Type 1 diesels, which were replaced with a further order for English Electric Class 20 engines, an older but proven design. Even so, Clayton Type 1 diesels became the new Shap bankers, but not for long. Withdrawal of the original characterful Derby 'lightweight' diesel multiple units proceeded quickly.

Also due for the axe were the almost new Class 14 Western Region 0-6-0 trip shunters, many of which were going into store. These engines were not troublesome, but the work for which they were designed was disappearing. It was reported that more than thirty were in store at Hull depot, which had received a big fleet of them from the Western Region. Many were sold to the National Coal Board and British Steel, who probably got a great bargain. A few, just three or four years old, were sold for scrap. The first three Swindon Warships, Nos D800–2, were withdrawn. The 'D' prefix was discontinued on diesels – it had been used to distinguish them from steam numbers. It was common to see trains in mixed liveries – a rake of maroon coaches with a couple of blue and grey ones inserted, or the other way round. Welcome to our colourful railways.

The Class EM2 electric fleet was withdrawn and replaced by Class 76 EM1 engines … but the writing was on the wall for the Sheffield–Manchester passenger trains. Another electric minor celebrity – No. E2001 – was moved to Akeman Street to be used for wind trials, before going to Rugby Testing Station, where it was stored. This had been built as No. 18100, a Western Region gas turbine engine.

BR repainted the Vale of Rheidol engines and stock in the new corporate blue livery, with a mixed reception. 'We want no history on our railway' was the clear message. The last regular steam-hauled express was a service from Preston to Blackpool South. The Scottish Region withdrew the last four observation cars.

1969 – Where Have All the Spotters Gone?

After the storm came the calm; these were the wilderness years. Once steam had disappeared, there was a vacuum in railway enthusiasm, which wasn't to be filled for some time. The hordes of youthful (and not so young) platform-enders seemed to have disappeared. Blue and grey coaches became the norm and much of the fascination of our railway heritage was missing after years of rationalisation and closures. The new idea of an unstaffed halt was about to proliferate and the local goods train became a much rarer event. Wagonload traffic, however, was to continue for many years adding variety to the railway scene. For enthusiasts in the Northampton area like me, it was the end of the ironstone railways; it seemed amazing that in only five years or so dozens of them had been swept away as a whole industry rapidly declined. Some steel works also switched to imported ore.

In 1969 the last trains ran over the Waverley Route from Carlisle to Scotland. A special hauled by a Deltic locomotive ran over the line on 5 January, allowing people to pay their last respects. Bold plans to save this line had been announced by the Border Union Railway Company, but in the end these came to nothing. The Beeching closures were almost complete, but a few lingered on, like the end of the Lewes–Uckfield line, closed in 1969. The Swanage branch also closed, as did the line from Wymondham to Dereham in East Anglia and a few other services. But the network was starting to settle down into something like its future shape and size.

There was a huge effort by projected heritage railways to acquire stock – especially the North York Moors, Severn Valley, Keighley and Worth Valley, Main Line Steam Trust (for the Great Central Railway), Stour Valley, and North Norfolk. All these lines were either working towards opening or had just opened. Barry scrapyard was now the focus of many eager eyes seeking motive power for the future. Rumours abounded that cutting up was due to start, but around 200 engines stood on the Welsh coast, many of them in good condition.

Among the withdrawals were the three Southern electrics – 20001–3 – which, like the five early diesels on the London Midland Region – 10000/1 and 10201–3 – were sadly scrapped. Diesel preservation only really got going with the loss of the Western Region hydraulics, which were actually a lot less significant than the engines listed above. The seven Class EM2 electric locomotives were sold to the Netherlands Railways – a good deal for both parties. The first of the North British Class 29 diesel-electrics was taken out of service; these were rebuilds of the hopeless Class 21 engines with a much better Paxman engine, but as a non-standard class they had no place in BR's future traction plans. The North British Class 22 diesel hydraulics were being rapidly withdrawn and the Class 28 Co-Bos became extinct. In contrast, some withdrawn North British 'Warship' Class 43 diesels were put back in traffic due to delays by the LMR in transferring Class 47s to the Western Region.

Flying Scotsman set off on its ill-fated American adventure and there was no steam at all running on British Rail, except the Vale of Rheidol narrow gauge line. Steam was still at work on industrial lines, but even this was becoming much rarer than five years previously. The Central Wales line, due for closure, was reprieved, but the graceful station at Manchester Central shut its doors for the last time.

1970 – Cider, Strikes and Speed

Local trains between Skipton and Carlisle were withdrawn in May and most of the intermediate stations closed. Both trains and stations on this, the Settle–Carlisle line, have been re-instated and today are very successful. The Cambridge to St Ives passenger service was also withdrawn.

No. 6000 *King George V*, safely in the care of H. P. Bulmer, was displayed to the public every weekend and operated on a lengthy siding. It was stage two in the return to steam story. A notable departure from Barry scrapyard was Somerset and Dorset 2-8-0 No. 53808, which left by rail. It was great to hear that a local ironstone engine, *Lamport No. 3*, had also been saved for preservation. A4 No. 60010 *Dominion of Canada* was restored at Crewe works and shipped to Canada for preservation.

The film *The Railway Children* was made at the Worth Valley line. The effects of its publicity have been beneficial to the line, and maybe railway preservation in general, ever since. The Severn Valley Railway opened for business as just a short section from Bridgnorth to Hampton Loade; I remember visiting it in the very early days and thinking what a wonderful project it was.

An especially interesting paper was released by BR about future high-speed trains and predicting the launch of the Inter City 125 Class 43 units. Many of the features mentioned appeared in the production units when they were delivered in 1975. Who would have believed these units would still be in front line service forty years later? Using pairs of Class 50 engines, the service from Crewe to Glasgow was speeded up as a prelude to electrification.

After the holocaust in the 1960s, the only withdrawals most months were diesel shunters – some of those being sold into industry. The nameplates carried by the Class 76 electrics used on the Woodhead route were sadly removed. It gave these old engines some character. Maybe BR wanted to raise a bit of income.

Agreement was reached to build a circular line through Liverpool connecting James Street, Moorfields, Lime Street, and Central. This replaced a terminus station at Central Low Level. Among a decreasing number of station closures, Narborough station in Leicestershire was actually re-opened following public protests. Yarmouth South Town, which once had a full express service to Liverpool Street, was quietly closed after years of decline.

This was also the start of a decade of strikes and disputes which brought the railways to their knees and gave the travelling public every excuse to find some other way of moving about the country.

1971 – An Old King Rules

In 1971 London Transport said goodbye to its last steam locomotives, which were ex-Western Region pannier tanks, apparently due partly to a lack of spare parts. Many of them ended up in preservation. In October, No. 6000 *King George V* surprised everyone by pulling a series of main-line specials to give hope to those yearning to see a future for steam on British Railways. I went to Banbury to watch this elegant engine pause for a few minutes and then head off towards Birmingham with its Pullman cars and it was a real pleasure to see steam at work once again. This was a feasibility exercise and led directly to the restoration of steam working on BR.

Trials started with automatic public address systems in trains, while more details of the forthcoming High Speed Trains were revealed. The Altrincham to Manchester line was converted from 1,500 volts DC to the standard 25 Kv AC electric power. Resignalling of the West Coast main line north of Weaver junction started in preparation for the start of electric services in 1973.

The last remaining section of the Stratford-upon-Avon and Midland Junction Railway from Fenny Compton station to Kineton military depot was taken over by the Army. Amazingly, it still exists today. Not important? The experience of Bryan and me in walking all the line in the 1960s and then watching it disappear certainly made it seem so.

British Railways proposed withdrawing services from the Bletchley–Bedford line, a battle that was fought and won by strong opposition. The Scottish Region announced that it planned to close the Kyle of Lochalsh line – happily this did not happen either. Southern 2-BIL and 2-HAL stock made their last runs and Butlins decided to dispose of its fleet of eight steam engines.

1972 – For Whom the Belle Tolls

It was the end for the lovely Brighton Belle, by now forty years old and showing its age compared to modern stock. There was a scramble to acquire these units by pubs and preservationists. Some years later I had my first meal on the Brighton Belle, sitting in a car park in Northern England. The last 4-COR Southern electric units, which had given such faithful service, were withdrawn. New deliveries included the 4-VEP and 4-CIG units.

One class rendered extinct was the LMS 350 hp diesel shunter (Class 11), withdrawals of which had started in 1967. They were precursors of the huge fleet of similar shunters purchased by BR. Among the Class 08 withdrawals was the very first one, No. 3000, which was sold to industry. I saw it at Worcester this year. Another class to bite the dust was the Western Region Warship, when the final four were taken out of service at the end of 1972. This left only five classes of named diesel locomotives in service – the Class 40, 45/46, 47, 52 and 55. Swindon also ceased overhauls on Class 52 Western diesels, hanging a guillotine over the class. Some of them were already confined to freight work. Many Hymeks were still active, but faced early withdrawal; in one month more than half the class was withdrawn. Also withdrawn was the Golden Arrow Pullman train.

A start was made on changing electric locomotives to TOPS numbers and the prototype Advanced Passenger Train made its appearance – what a shame that it was left to the Italian Pendolino to capitalise on all that endeavour and know-how.

Matlock Bath station re-opened, having closed five years previously. A good decision, as it attracted 60,000 grateful passengers in 2015. Passenger services from Penrith to Keswick were withdrawn, the premature end of a wonderful railway.

The programme to bring back steam to BR was called 'Return to Steam' and followed the successful trials with *King George V* in 1971. Two or three trains were planned each month using a variety of engines including *Bittern*, LMS Class 5 No. 4932, *Bahamas*, *Sir Nigel Gresley*, and *Clan Line*. Five routes were agreed for steam use and twenty-three locomotives listed as approved to run trains, although some were still in the process of repairs or overhauls. The first specials were run in June. We went to the newly opened Birmingham Museum of Science and Industry to see No. 46235 *City of Birmingham* move a few feet along a piece of track – she looked wonderful, but like a caged bull. Rebuilt SR Pacifics *City of Wells* and *Bodmin* departed from Barry with about forty engines in the yard reserved or already in new ownership.

Bristol Parkway station was opened, setting a new trend for stations outside towns near strategic road junctions. New special use bulk wagons and air-conditioned Mark 2D stock started service on the London Midland Region.

1973 – 'Hey – Let's Buy a Steam Engine'

Trials commenced with the new Class 252 High Speed Train units following a delay as the union ASLEF, true to form, had banned any involvement with it (and the ATP prototype). When it did get going the HST showed its potential by achieving 141 mph. The Class 41 HST was a very significant newcomer as it foreshadowed a world where nearly all passenger trains would be some kind of fixed formation multiple unit. Derby Research Centre had three interesting withdrawn locomotives on its books at the time – D832 *Onslaught*, Metrovick Co-Bo No. D5705, and Baby Deltic No. D5901. I saw two of these when on a train passing through Derby that year, but sadly it was not possible to get a photograph, although I did picture the Class 41 HST unit. The first diesels with TOPS numbers also appeared. Trials started in service with the Southern 4-PEP unit No. 4001. Another significant newcomer was the pioneer Class 87 electric locomotive No. 87001, which I saw being towed through Crewe station in May. Outmoded by more modern forms of coaching stock, the Blue Pullmans were withdrawn by BR with hardly a tear. Our local scrapyard at Kettering was busy torching 350 bhp diesel shunters and Hymeks.

The benefits of the council-dominated PTEs were starting to appear with bold plans to increase services after years of contraction, and BR itself was focusing on improving Inter-City services. Yet Bradford Exchange, a lovely old building that deserved a better fate, saw its last trains and its replacement, the soulless Interchange station, welcomed its first customers. A bright idea from BR was to create a special train for football fans with such vehicles as a disco coach, TV coach and two coaches with music; presumably there was a fighting saloon as well. Anyway, it was rapidly booked for lots of special workings.

Steam special trains started running on the Scarborough line with one of them hauled by A4 No.19 *Bittern*; we sometimes forget that this engine had a short previous life on the main line. Among preservation news items was the repatriation of a WD 2-8-0 from Sweden. You can see it today as 90733 at the Worth Valley line. The Main Line Steam Trust had started its Great Central Railway project by leasing Loughborough station and acquiring Pacific No. 34039 *Boscastle* from Barry. They launched services on the double track between Loughborough and Quorn and Woodhouse using a Black Five in September 1973.

Another Southern Pacific, No. 35005 *Canadian Pacific*, went to Carnforth. Meanwhile, a group buying No. 6024 *King Edward I* from Barry for £4,000 revealed that restoration would cost only £10,000! Some hope. *Flying Scotsman*'s disastrous adventure abroad was over – the engine was purchased by Sir William McAlpine with a view to its going on display at the new York museum. I saw it standing outside Derby Works, looking very tired, but happily back on these shores. *Railway World* magazine, which always specialised in history and preservation, reported forty-eight preservation projects in the UK, from museums to complete railways. The Paignton to Kingswear line re-opened as a steam railway on 1 January; this was an interesting project as BR basically handed over a working line for the Dart Valley Railway to run. Hall 4-6-0 No. 4942 *Maindy Hall* was purchased for conversion to a Saint 4-6-0 – a project still under way forty years later. A foolhardy group announced they wanted to buy and restore Pacific No. 71000 *Duke of Gloucester* (as if such a thing were possible!). The doubters were made to eat their words.

1974 – Switch on the Juice

With the significant exception of the opening of full electric services from Euston to Glasgow, 1974 was a quiet year. About an hour was saved over previous Anglo–Scottish journey times. This led to the movement of many Class 50 engines to the Western Region, although fifteen stayed in the north to handle freight. The National Coal Board launched a major investment in equipment for merry-go-round coal trains.

Spots and spotlights were in the news – certain engines received headlights, while others had their head code numbers replaced by a black panel and two large white dots. Work had started to build the production series of High Speed Trains following successful trials with the prototype. This was the big year for renumbering of the BR diesel fleet, with some rather neat old style numbers, like Peak No. 1 *Scafell Pike,* disappearing in favour of new class identities. Hymeks, Westerns and shunters were the main classes withdrawn; new engines comprised just the Class 87 electrics. Magazines reported that D601 *Ark Royal,* one of only two diesels at Barry, was to be preserved. Alas ... Meanwhile, the Brush Falcon diesel led a precarious life, but was eventually returned to service.

Among the more ambitious preservation schemes approaching fruition was the West Somerset Railway; Pacific No. 71000 *Duke of Gloucester* actually left Barry to defy the doubters and Class N 2-6-0 No. 31874 was purchased and restored by John Bunch, who I believe still owns it today. This was also the year of the Great Western Society's amazing vintage train – a sight we shall not witness again.

1975 – I've Seen the Future and it's Called HST

A number of principal express trains, including the Thames-Clyde Express, the Emerald Isle Express, and the Devonian, lost their names. Having survived a closure threat, the Kyle of Lochalsh line looked set for extra freight traffic.

Extensive engineering work was carried out on both the East Coast route and the South Wales main line ready for the introduction of the HST services. In contrast, there were still plenty of mixed freights around with varying wagons, some of them trundling along lonely branches that once carried passengers as well. It would not last forever. The first 75-foot-long Mark 3 coaches for the London Midland Region entered service; it was amazing how big they seemed compared with previous stock. It was reported that thirty-five extra Leeds–Bradford trains were to be introduced each day – a sign of how PTEs were getting to grips with local rail services.

Rumours of the death of the Hymeks continued, yet a handful of these engines continued in service. I was a regular visitor to Birmingham New Street around this time and Western diesels were making regular visits, although withdrawals of this much-loved class were under way. A start was also made on scrapping the Class 24 diesels. Some diesel multiple units were refurbished and repainted in white livery and the final Class 87 – No. 87101 – was delivered.

The new National Railway Museum at York was opened – not without some complaints from those who thought it should remain in the capital. The Rail150 Cavalcade, created to celebrate 150 years since the opening of the Stockton and Darlington Railway, featured thirty-five locomotives, including the biggest gathering of steam locomotives since the end of steam on BR. More than a thousand miles of BR track were open to steam in 1975. No. 6229 *Duchess of Hamilton* was moved to Swindon for restoration as a static exhibit for the new railway museum at York and locomotives were pouring out of Barry. In those days Barry engines were 'repaired' or 'overhauled' – soon afterwards the word 'rebuilt' was being used. Not every scheme made it, though; among projects that went nowhere was one to repatriate a Great Central 2-8-0 from Australia. The only LNER engine at Barry, B1 No. 61264, was saved and when I saw it I thought: 'They'll never get that running.' As we know now, this was the age of mission impossible. By the end of 1975, seventy-eight engines had left Barry, and Dai Woodham, the yard's owner, was a minor celebrity. If your preservation scheme needed an ex-Barry Castle 4-6-0, sorry, you were too late. Two interesting old engines back in steam were Great Northern Atlantic No. 990 *Henry Oakley* and the veteran LNWR 2-4-0 *Hardwicke*.

Twenty years had elapsed since the publication of that famous modernisation plan. While huge progress had been made, in the end the key achievement in the years from 1965 to 1975 was to set the scene for the future – a world of electrification, HSTs and various types of multiple units. The world, in fact, that we have today. For the railway enthusiast, it was a fascinating time; steam had returned and stations were again a source of interest from a new army of railfans, only this time they were called 'gricers.' (I wonder why?). Yet, when I asked a non-enthusiast to read this text to see if she found it interesting, she could hardly believe it.

'You mean they really scrapped all those almost-new diesels?'

'Growing pains,' I said dryly.

Here we see the late afternoon express for Euston arriving at Northampton Castle station. In charge on 20 September 1965 is English Electric Type 4 (later Class 40) No. D303. Notice the motley collection of rolling stock (the first two coaches are non-corridor) and the boy in his Eaglehurst College striped jacket – where I went to school. The station is partly rebuilt and the wires are up for the imminent electrification.

The best of steam. We had saved up all our precious pennies to purchase tickets on the Bournemouth Belle and Nine Elms shed did us proud by producing a very clean Merchant Navy 4-6-2, No. 35011 *General Steam Navigation*. We are about to board for Bournemouth West – it's 8 June 1965 and the end of Southern steam feels a very long way away, but in just over two years No. 35011, the Bournemouth Belle and its destination station will be history.

On 20 September 1965, Class 8F 2-8-0 No. 48637 blasts through Northampton Castle station with a northbound freight in the late afternoon sun. I seem to be trespassing!

Racing north through the lovely Derbyshire station at Cromford is Crosti 9F 2-10-0 No. 92022 on its way to Manchester. Just look at the gardens full of flowers. Today the station is open, but with just a single track and its elegance lost. This was a lovely summer's day, 3 August 1965, and it seemed as though such scenes would last forever.

A Northampton 8F 2-8-0, No. 48449, works an electrification engineering train north through Castle station on 12 June 1965. The station is being rebuilt and you can clearly see the join between the old and the new in this picture. There was always a sense of doom about these trains, as though the old stager was helping with its own demise.

As electrification forced its way south, steam retrenched, but not in an orderly way. By 3 August 1965, when this picture at Nuneaton was taken, some sheds south of here were about to close, yet this one worked with steam through to mid-1966. Seen here are Class 4 4-6-0 No. 75043 from Aintree and local Stanier 8F No. 48206.

Leaving Northampton Castle station on 12 May 1966 is a London Euston to Coventry service comprising a new Class AM10 EMU, No. 067. Derby Works delivered fifty of these units in a shade of blue that was darker and more elegant than the later 'rail blue.' They gave many years of excellent service. Notice the bags of mail on the platform and the station under reconstruction.

On 4 June 1966 a young signalman at Rockingham station has come down from his box to watch the progress of the 12.40 Harwich–Rugby through train using the Rugby–Peterborough line for the last time. In charge is a newly-painted Type 2 diesel, No. D5145. Even the buffers look little used. Only the weeds in the track suggest this is the last day for traffic on this line.

Here we are at Stamford Town and the train in the bay is for Seaton. Notice the sign advertising cheap trips – Clacton is 34 shillings (equivalent to £1.70 in today's money). I can see I am reflected in the front window. This is a Class 100 Gloucester RCW diesel multiple unit, which carries a steam-age rear oil lamp. (4 June 1966).

You can see the M1 bridge in the background as a pair of BRCW Class 104 three-car sets arrive at Lilbourne on their way to Rugby Midland on 4 June 1966. There are plenty of people in the cab; passengers had a fine view through the cab windows in these units. The old angled Hawkseye LMS name boards were a feature of some stations on this line. Even today you can just glimpse the derelict platforms of this station if you glance along the track bed from the motorway.

Passengers no more – a poignant sight all too familiar throughout Britain in the mid-1960s. This is Thrapston Bridge Street station in June 1966, two years after passenger services between Northampton and Peterborough were axed by Dr Beeching. It gave service to the town for 120 years and, like most of the elegant stations on this line, was designed by John Livock. (Bryan Jeyes)

The driver of this BR diesel-hydraulic Hymek diesel (Class 35), No. D7051, looks very happy to be photographed at Banbury station as he moves a freight train slowly past on 8 August 1966. The engine looks far from smart and was withdrawn in the early 1970s. That first van looks like an old horse box. This was a class that was condemned under the *National Traction Plan*.

Sleeping through the afternoon at Northampton Castle station on a bright 12 May 1966 are these two English Electric Type 4 diesels (Class 40), Nos D305 and D293. This siesta was a fairly regular occurrence for a few months. D293 is much the cleaner. These heavy engines only held control of the West Coast main line top link services from 1961 to 1965.

A grubby Class 5 4-6-0 No. 44776 waits to leave Banbury General with a northbound parcels train on 8 June 1966. The Western Region had already eliminated steam, but in areas like Banbury, which had been transferred to the London Midland Region, steam hung on for a few months longer.

Right until 1967 you could still find steam on the Cambrian main line, restricted to certain passenger services. Standard Class 4 4-6-0 No. 75012 is leaving Portmadoc station with the Pwlheli portion of the Cambrian Coast Express on 23 October 1966. Early in 1967 diesels took over completely and No. 75012 was withdrawn. Amazingly, she moved depots five times during 1966, surely some kind of record. (Bryan Jeyes)

A last day brake van special on the Cromford and High Peak Railway – an unlikely survivor into the 1960s. The two regular Class J94 0-6-0 saddle tanks, Nos 68006 and 68012, have been smartened up for a last day special. Today the track bed is a cycle and walking trail. (Bryan Jeyes)

The Class AL5 (later 85) engines were the BR-built version of the Type A electrics. Here we see No. E3068 in its original electric blue livery standing in the bay at Northampton Castle station (Platform 2, I think) while parcels are loaded behind it on 12 April 1966.

This engine, No. E3147, is brand new and is grinding to a halt at Northampton Castle station on 12 May 1966, with a red light ahead. It later became No. 86211 *City of Milton Keynes* but was written off after a crash. Again, this shows the original blue livery of Class AL6 – less bright than the electric blue of the older engines and with the elegant raised number and crest. Despite its recent construction, No. E3147 is on a pretty lowly duty. The preceding freight can be seen heading under Spencer Bridge.

Heading south with a freight is BR Class 25 Sulzer diesel No. D7551. The train is just approaching Lamport station on the Market Harborough–Northampton line on 24 June 1966 and she looks none too clean. This line clung to life for many years, even though local passenger services had been withdrawn in 1960. It finally felt the axe in 1981.

Roaring through Fenny Compton on the Paddington–Birmingham main line is a Banbury 9F, No. 92228, with a mixed freight. The lifted line on the right is the old Stratford-upon-Avon and Midland Junction route to Towcester, which had been taken up a few weeks before. 23 June 1966.

A year earlier this would have been a job for a Jinty 3F tank. Now, on 12 May 1966, we have 0-6-0 shunter No. D3068 heading a short freight of tank wagons from Far Cotton to Spencer Bridge yard 'wrong way' through Northampton Castle station, a very unusual occurrence. The guy in the brake van looks very unconcerned and the yard looks busy. This engine – and LMS 'jackshaft' 0-6-0 No. 12009 – were newcomers.

On 12 May 1966, Class AL6 electric No. E3188 approaches a red light at Northampton station. The 'new railway' is fully working – this was a day of endless freights through Northampton. The wagons are deceptively old – they were built in 1929 for the LMS to carry coal to the power station at Stonebridge Park.

You may recognise this as Shrewsbury station. We were here in the pouring rain on 21 August 1966, the start of a week's holiday in Wales photographing trains. We had hoped for some steam at Shrewsbury, but the only train present was this one, headed by Brush Type 4 (Class 47) No. D1587. Notice the red spot under the number, Great Western steam style.

Among all the electric-hauled freights at Northampton Castle station came this mixed load headed by an English Electric Type 4 diesel (Class 40) No. D305, already demoted from passenger work. The remains of the old LNWR island platform building are being demolished; behind this, the new construction has been completed, with West Bridge visible in the background. The rebuilding of the West Coast main line for electrification, which involved raising the height of many bridges, was an enormous engineering task. 12 May 1966.

Heading south at Wellingborough Midland Road on 20 September 1966 is an express headed by Class 25 diesel No. D5195.The train is the 12.06 Bradford Forster Square– St Pancras which sometimes had a modest Type 2 in charge. This was a very hot day for late September and perfect for photography. It was the last year when you could see both steam and diesels on the Midland main line south of Leicester. The classic Midland signal box with its fire buckets survived until 1987; the steam age water crane and a cluster of semaphore signals add to the scene.

A lucky catch by photographer Terry Campbell at Healey Mills yard – Class 25 D5242 tows preserved Jubilee 4-6-0 No. 45596 *Bahamas* from Stockport to the Hunslet Engine Co. in Leeds for repairs on 29 September 1967. The yard looks busy with plenty of Class 40s and 37s evident. (Terry Campbell)

Action at Wakefield Kirkgate station in July 1967, with a four-car Metro-Cammell diesel unit about to pass Brush Type 2 No. D5653. A burst of steam in the distance shows the dinosaur still lives. (Bob Mullins)

Racing through Hook at high speed on a down Bournemouth express is a very shabby rebuilt Battle of Britain 4-6-2 No. 34077 *603 Squadron*. The date is 4 March 1967 and although running well with a top link express, this engine was withdrawn for scrap three weeks later on 26 March. She has a crude wooden numberplate and Eastleigh shed obviously hasn't cleaned her for a long time.

Merchant Navy Pacific No. 35003 *Royal Mail* hardly looks ready for the breaker's yard as it backs on to a train for Bournemouth at Waterloo early in 1967. On 26 June that year, in a final fling of speed, No. 35003 reached 106 mph. A few days later she was withdrawn for scrap. (Bryan Jeyes)

An atmospheric picture which says everything about the death of the steam era in 1967. This is Wakefield shed, with an 8F trundling past cooling towers and a row of redundant steam engines. These were the dying days for steam, which by now was confined just to the north of England. (Bob Mullins)

A rather sad line up at Rose Grove shed on 10 March 1968 with a few months left before the end. Awaiting removal are, from left to right, two Stanier 8F 2-8-0s (probably 48310 and 48468) along with Standard Class 4 4-6-0 No. 75032. No. 48310 appears to have a full tender, which certainly won't be needed. (Terry Campbell)

On 25 March 1968 at Mirfield in Yorkshire, Stanier 8F 2-8-0 No. 48384 returns light engine to Rose Grove after bringing a freight across the Pennines to Healey Mills. Steam has only a few months to run. (Terry Campbell)

Here we are at the South Durham system of quarries at Irchester, Northamptonshire, on 10 February 1968. The Hawthorn Leslie 0-4-0ST Holwell No. 30 is coming uphill with a fully loaded train of iron ore. She was cut up nearby at the Cransley yard of George Cohen the following year (one of three sent there) after the system closed on 27 June 1969. In ten years the huge local ironstone industry had virtually disappeared.

Birmingham Railway Carriage and Wagon Co. Type 2 No. D5335 at Inverness shed on 6 August 1969. She was the last green Class 26 by quite some margin, not being painted blue until late 1973. This very useful class did sterling work in the Scottish Region. (Gordon Edgar)

Hasty purchasing leads to bad decision making. Metrovick Class 28 Co-Bo No. D5712 is seen at Reddish depot on 26 May 1968. It was withdrawn in September that year and subsequently cut up at J. Cashmore, Great Bridge, during December 1969. The Metrovick, arguably the worst type of diesel ever bought by a British railway, is surrounded by Class EM1 electrics. (Gordon Edgar)

Another pilot scheme failure. North British Type 2s Nos D6130 and D6137 stand alongside BRCW Type 2 No. 5357 at Eastfield depot on 10 August 1969. The North British pair had been rebuilt in 1965 with replacement Paxman power units and reclassified as Class 29, but only remained in service until 1971. Both were cut up during 1972 at BREL Glasgow. (Gordon Edgar)

On a clear cold February day, Class 40 No. D347 of Healey Mills and Class 24 D5147 of Holbeck are seen running as light engines towards Stourton. Both these types gave reasonable service to British Railways, but were soon outclassed by more modern types and changing traffic patterns. This picture was taken at Leeds Holbeck on 17 February 1969. (Terry Campbell)

Gordon Edgar, on a visit to BR Swindon Works on 5 August 1970, found pilot scheme Warship class diesel-hydraulics Nos D801 *Vanguard* and D802 *Formidable* in contrasting liveries being cannibalised for spares. Rated at 2,000 horse power (instead of the standard 2,200 hp for the remainder of the class), the first three Warships D800 – D802 were early candidates for withdrawal. These were the first two of the class to be dispatched at Swindon Works during October of that year, following retrieval of any useful parts. D800 had been dealt with at Cashmores, Newport, during the previous year, all three being just twelve years old. (Gordon Edgar)

The revival of the Severn Valley line was a major event in railway preservation; here we see Class 2 2-6-0 No. 46443 at Hampton Loade on 6 September 1970. These modern 2-6-0s were to become one of the more useful types for preserved railways, being cheap to run, easy to service, and able to cope with the modest loads used on most heritage lines.

It's 1971 and for British Rail, the Class 14 saga is over. Ex-BR No. D9555, still in its original livery, is seen at Burradon with a load from Weetslade Coal Preparation Plant on 1 September 1971. D9555 was delivered new from Swindon in October 1965, but was sold out of BR service in April 1969 and acquired by the National Coal Board for use on the Ashington system. Even as these engines were being built, the work destined for them evaporated. (Gordon Edgar)

Time of change. We are at the south end of Wellingborough station on 23 August 1971. The closed Northampton branch line heads off to the right, while approaching from the south is Class 45 No. 54 *The Royal Pioneer Corps*. The 'D' prefix was fast disappearing from diesels.

On 17 April 1971 I am at Roade, where the Northampton and Rugby lines separate. This parcels train, hauled by a Class 85 engine, is coming in from Northampton, with the main line from Rugby in the foreground.

A busy early morning scene at Newton Abbot on 19 June 1971. I have arrived on the overnight sleeper from Birmingham (pictured right). Western diesel No. D1022 *Western Sentinel* leaves for Paddington. Blue and grey have taken over completely.

Wellingborough Finedon Road on 23 August 1971. Over the years I have taken quite a few shots here and each one shows a more rationalised view. At this time, the yard was still busy. Telegraph poles, semaphore signals, unfitted mineral wagons – not much had changed in the past ten years except for steam yielding to this attractive engine, No. D5234.

Rushing north along the Midland main line at Irchester on 23 August 1971 is an express headed by Brush Type 4 No. 1651, still in green livery. These engines seemed to be everywhere during the 1970s.

Today we take regular steam on the main line for granted. But this was the train that started it all – No. 6000 *King George V* and the Bulmer's Pullman cars. It is heading into Banbury on a very gloomy day, 15 August 1971. A surprisingly small number of people were present – maybe its journey was not widely known. For me, it was a pilgrimage.

Class 1400 No. 1420
runs round its train
on 8 September 1971
on the Dart Valley
Railway. The old Devon
Belle observation car is
a handsome survivor
of a golden age that
had disappeared on
British Rail.

On 11 September
1971, I am watching a
train curving round
from Paignton to
Torquay. In charge is
Class 47 No. 1903 in
green livery with a
heavy fourteen-coach
load heading for the
Eastern Region.

I think we can safely
say this is a scene
not envisaged by
the proponents of a
modern new railway.
On 12 September
1971, surrounded by
cranes building a new
Carlsberg Brewery,
a train crosses
Northampton Bridge
Street, the site of an
old station. In charge
is Sulzer Type 2
No. 7641 and the load
will be coal for the
power station.

On 15 July 1972 at Greetland/West Vale, near Halifax, English Electric Type 3 No. 6926 of Tinsley passes on a Sheffield–Blackpool summer Saturday train. In the foreground is the very short branch to a small oil terminal. (Terry Campbell)

This Metro-Cammell multiple unit is standing at Peterborough North and is waiting to depart for Cambridge on 4 February 1972. Later this year, the dreaded 20 mph speed restriction through the station that had blighted express trains for years was eliminated when the track layout was remodelled.

They were always trying to close the Bletchley–Bedford line, but happily never succeeded. In 1972 it looked as though the writing was on the wall, so we spent a day travelling on the branch taking photographs. This is Stewartby, the site of the main London Brick Works site along the line, and you can see the forest of chimneys pouring out smelly purple clag. There were chimneys on both sides of the line with a bridge linking the two sites, just visible in the distance.

Arriving at Truro station with Presflo wagons is Warship No. 807 *Caradoc* on 12 September 1972. By this time the short-lived Warship class was almost history, but *Caradoc* is in quite nice condition.

The delightful station at Stamford Town is seen here on 7 July 1972 with a Swindon DMU on a service heading for Peterborough.

In many places the old railway still survived in 1972. A Cravens DMU holds up the traffic (one Ford Cortina with a learner driver!) as it leaves Lidlington station and heads west to Bletchley from Bedford on 8 December 1972. Notice the child standing on the gate.

English Electric Class 20 diesels Nos 8003 and 8196 in a scene that is a real mixture of the old and the new. The row of empty mineral wagons with a brake van and the industrial plant (Old Cross Dyeworks) emitting steam smack of years gone by. The colour light signals and diesel locomotives indicate a more modern railway. The picture was taken at Stapleford on 29 October 1972 and both engines are painted blue.

My notes say that the Brush Type 4 is heading a Kings Cross to Cleethorpes train, just leaving Grantham station on 7 July 1972. In the bay is a DMU with a connecting service to Skegness. This was my only visit to Grantham – my usual East Coast route haunts were Kings Cross, Sandy, Peterborough, and Doncaster. The locomotive is in green livery.

Nine tracks and five engines at Toton MPD on 26 October 1972. All were stalwarts of this big depot at the time. On the left we have a BR Class 25, No. 7615, then Class 20 No. 8067, another unidentified Class 20, then Peak Class 45 No. 54 *The Royal Pioneer Corps* and finally another Class 25. The 'D' prefix seems to have gone completely. The air was thick with the sound and smell of idling diesels.

A train of tank wagons heads south from Wellingborough behind a Class 47 diesel in 1972. The location is the erstwhile junction of the Higham Ferrers branch, here lifted, but offering an unusual location for photography.

Passing through Peterborough North station on 4 February 1972 is a Brush Type 2 locomotive on a short freight, which is taking the line to March. The engine, No. D5524, is still painted green and is one of the early ones with no head code panel.

When I first glanced at this slide I had absolutely no memory of taking this picture, and certainly could not identify the location. Luckily I am fairly diligent when it comes to writing down dates, so I know that No. 1583 is at Gloucester Eastgate on 31 August 1972. The station was closed three years later and is now the site of an Asda supermarket.

On 7 July 1972 a Swindon Inter-City DMU races through Kings Sutton station in Northamptonshire. These later became Class 123 and they added to the tremendous variety of different trains you could see back in the early 1970s. Amazingly this tiny station survives to this day.

On a misty morning (26 October 1972) I went to Radcliffe-on-Soar, which was a great place to watch trains on the Midland main line. Here we see the power station looming over a BR Sulzer Type 2, No. D7556, which is trundling south with six bogie hopper wagons, just as the sun is debating whether or not to appear. This picture shows how effective the all yellow front end is as a warning device. Aesthetically it is a disaster, however, and in the United States – where I lived for many years – a front spotlight and a horn were deemed sufficient as a warning, even with all their level crossings.

Tamworth High Level is a very dull station architecturally. It had a steeply graded line running down to the low-level station where I once saw a Fowler 4F in all kinds of trouble trying to move a freight uphill, tender first. No such problems for Peak No. 187, which is moving away after stopping with a Newcastle–Weymouth service on 28 July 1972.

I am now at Toton and these English Electric Type 1 diesels were everywhere. I took this portrait of No. 8141 moving slowly past to the shed on 26 October 1972. These engines proved a good investment by BR, even with their visibility problems for the crew when running forwards.

We are at Beeston, near Nottingham, for this shot, with Class 45 No. 120 heading through the station on a dull October day. The station still has the 'sausage' totems; a fascinating selection of cars fills the parking area. (29 October 1972)

This view was taken looking north from the over bridge near Wellingborough station. On this day – 19 November 1972 – a Class 47 in green livery, No. 1779, is braking for a stop at the station. The engine shed has received a new roof (it still exists today) and while the clusters of 9Fs have gone, the place still looks fairly busy.

At this time, all the first ten Peak locomotives were rumbling around Nottinghamshire on coal trains, although I did see one at Northampton during this period. Here, on 26 October 1972, the class leader No. 1 *Scafell Pike* rests between duties at Toton depot – a very small number for a very large locomotive. These were some of the more successful pilot scheme diesels.

The interest for me in this picture is the over bridge, which is situated south of the old Melton Mowbray North station (by this time, demolished). A Type 2 Sulzer, No. 7654, one of the later engines, has a freight in tow, taking the Leicester line on 7 July 1972. Melton Mowbray offered lots of great places to photograph trains, and ten years earlier would have been better still, with the main line to Nottingham and summer trains from Leicester Belgrave Road on the GN and LNWR Joint Line adding to the interest. I believe this bridge has now been removed.

This view will be familiar to many at Shrewsbury and No. D3870 is busy shunting coaches. This was 30 July 1972 and I was on my way home to Northampton. BR found employment for more than a thousand of these shunters at this time.

Outside Derby Research Centre on 1 September 1972 is the newly built prototype HST Class 252 set with its Mark 3 carriages. I think this set had not yet entered service due to its being blacked by the unions, so this is quite an interesting picture, even though it was taken from a passing train. Derby was a fascinating place through the 1950s, '60s and early '70s.

A scene at Leicester station on 1 September 1972 that had not changed much since steam days. The engine shed is in the distance and there are plenty of semaphore signals. Throbbing away on the left is a northbound express in the hands of Peak Type 4 No. D59 *The Royal Warwickshire Fusiliers*. Looking at this picture forty years later, I can almost hear the big engine rumbling away with that oily smell.

A peaceful setting at Worcester, with Class 47 No. 1612 awaiting its next duty. In the background a motley collection of condemned BR Mark 1 stock awaits its fate. A Class 25 keeps the Brush Type 4 company on 29 July 1972.

This is a train you could reproduce on a model railway – it only has a handful of wagons. The venue is Toton on 29 October 1972 and No. 8137 is taking it nice and easy; not a working that was going to survive in the new age of BR.

On 7 July 1972 I was at Little Bytham to watch trains. Heading past at high speed is Deltic No. 9009 *Alycidon* in very nice condition with a smart rake of blue and grey stock, mainly Mark 2D air-conditioned. The service is the 11.00 Edinburgh to Kings Cross. Notice the telegraph poles and semaphore signal – signs of our old railway. Alycidon was one of the most successful racehorses of the twentieth century and sired Meld (Deltic No. 9003).

Late afternoon at Coventry station and we see a long-lived Class AL6 locomotive, No. E3129, on a Wolverhampton service. This particular engine was eventually renumbered 86701 and was sold to Bulgaria where I gather it is still in service. This shot has a very '70s feel about it – it was taken on 30 July 1972.

A Brush Class 31 diesel, No. 5854, runs through Melton Mowbray light engine on 7 July 1972. Nothing much had changed in this scene for many years except for a coat of blue paint over engine and station.

At this time (29 July 1972) Hymeks worked many of the trains between Worcester and Paddington. I joined this late-afternoon service as far as Oxford, then caught a train to Leamington and eventually worked my way back to Northampton using my London Midland Region 'runabout' ticket. Here, the train is waiting to leave Worcester with No. 7009 up front.

Northampton station was often used to stable diesel and electric locomotives in the 1960s and 1970s and elsewhere in this book you can see two English Electric Type 4s in exactly this spot. But on 30 July 1972 this pair of first generation electrics, Nos 84003 and 83009, both in nice condition, are resting between duties. Notice the yard still has rows of old box vans. In some ways the modern railway had not yet arrived. TOPS numbers were very rare at this time.

Here's a busy locomotive. In this view, No. 1856 has a train of pipes passing Beeston, near Nottingham, on 26 October 1972 – but I photographed it again two weeks later at Wellingborough. The Shipstone's Maltings building was very prominent alongside the railway at this point.

These English Electric Type 3 engines became ubiquitous over the system and here we have one, No. 6864, running into Derby light engine on 1 September 1972. This was another type of engine that has proved excellent in service, with some still working fifty years after they were built. I believe this engine has only recently been withdrawn.

This is one of my favourite pictures, but I'm not sure why. I think it's the combination of a nice set of signals, a locomotive still with the small warning panel, and a lovely summer afternoon. The picture was taken at Melton Mowbray on 7 July 1972 and the engine is Class 25 No. 7647. It was one of the last three engines to retain its small warning panel. The sheeted wagons are a real thing of the past.

Shunters don't often look very attractive, but No. 3870 is doing its best here in a new coat of rail blue – a colour that looked okay when first applied, but quickly faded to a dreary dull bluey grey. She's been through Derby Works and I seem to remember a Baby Deltic being there, but I could not photograph it. She's a locally shedded engine so has been given the full treatment. 1 September 1972.

Heading north at Wellingborough on the Midland slow line on 10 November 1972 is a Peak diesel with a train of tank wagons. No. D109 is moving quite slowly in the late afternoon sunshine. That must be Rushden church on the skyline.

If you like Peak diesels, then here is a sight to please you at Leicester London Road station on 1 September 1972. I caught a train at Derby headed by ex-works Class 45 No. 76 (left). It was quite a surprise when we reached Leicester and No. 76 was removed, to be replaced for the journey southwards by sister engine No. 100 *Sherwood Forester*. This engine was also ex-works. The 11.50 Derby to St Pancras stopper was often used to run in overhauled engines.

The engine farthest from the camera is interesting, because it is the very first Class 08 shunter – No. 3000 built in 1953. She is seen here undergoing attention at Worcester shed on 29 July 1972 alongside a much newer classmate, No. 4120. No. 3000 is still with us, as she was preserved. No. 4120 was built ten years later and withdrawn in the early 1990s.

On 4 April 1972, Fowler Class 4F No. 3924 awaits its next duty at Haworth on the Keighley and Worth Valley Railway. There were plenty of engines in steam on this day. This 4F was the first engine to leave Barry scrapyard and was quickly returned to service; at the time of writing it is still in regular use.

We are now among the trainspotters at Birmingham New Street and a pair of Peak diesels has arrived at this great interchange station. On the left is No. 103 of Class 45 and on the right No. 151, one of the Class 46 variety. Both these engines survived until the mid-1980s. This scene was taken on 1 September 1972. It was the age of change – one of the spotters is a girl! No. 151 appears to have a screen wiper problem. Train 1M88 is the 06.25 Plymouth to Liverpool Lime Street and 1E54 is the 08.45 Cardiff to Leeds.

Southbound on the Settle–Carlisle line, with just a mile to run to Settle station, comes Class 40 No. 264 on a train of empty fitted mineral wagons. The date is 5 April 1972 and the time is late afternoon.

Here's something of a rarity. Outside the locomotive testing station at Rugby on 10 July 1972 is electric locomotive No. E2001. This was built as No. 18100 – a gas turbine engine – and was then rebuilt as an a.c. electric for crew training and testing. It was originally numbered E1000. I'd heard it was in Rugby testing station and was delighted to see it outside, ready for removal for scrap; I'll leave you to identify the cars!

I am back at one of my regular locations – the Irthlingborough road bridge at Wellingborough. An Up coal train rumbles past on 10 November 1972 with the familiar town skyline in the background. No. 1856 is in respectably clean green livery. We get a good view of the Morris Engines cylinder block foundry and its rail connection.

Heading east at Melton Mowbray is a Brush Type 2, No. 5680, on a train of ballast from Croft to Leyton. I am standing on the bridge that carried the old LNWR and GN joint line (to Melton Mowbray North) and the spotless permanent way adds to the scene. In the far distance you can just make out the huge Waltham-on-the-Wolds TV mast that was such a helpful landmark to me in my private flying days (it was unmissable – but beware in bad visibility!). The contents of the hopper wagons seem to match the ballast. The date is 7 July 1972.

Derby's painters have clearly done a great job here. No. 177, one of the Class 46 engines, is moving very slowly past the familiar background at Derby station on 1 September 1972. Taking pictures of ex-works engines was always fun but, living miles from the nearest works, I found it was an all-too rare treat for my camera.

The decision to axe the main line between Derby and Manchester came as a shock. When I visited Matlock on 28 July 1972 it had lost its sense of importance. My previous visits had been when it was part of a busy trunk line; now it was a feeble, unkempt branch. A Swindon DMU stands in the station and you can see the familiar hilly landscape behind the station with Riber Castle on the skyline. The station is much busier now, as Peak Rail are using the right hand platform for their heritage trains.

This is a location that has changed beyond imagination today. The houses in the background indicate an urban setting and in fact these two Type 1 diesels on a northbound freight are passing over a level crossing just outside Northampton – I think it is Boughton Crossing. The head code 8D57 suggests a through freight for North Wales. The date is 29 September 1972 and, just north of this area, the Northampton and Lamport Railway plans to come south from its base at Chapel Brampton. At the moment, the railway is a long way from either Northampton or Lamport, but they have ambitious plans. The engines are Nos 8168 and 8182.

More East Coast route action on 7 August 1972. Racing through Grantham station at very high speed is Deltic locomotive No. 9003 *Meld* and this low angle gives it a menacing appearance. She was named after the racehorse Meld, which won the 1,000 Guineas and the Epsom Oaks in 1955, before also winning the St Leger Stakes at Doncaster. The train is running from Kings Cross to Aberdeen.

After being rescued from Barry scrapyard, rebuilt West Country Pacific No. 34016 *Bodmin* went first of all to Quainton Road, where it is seen on 29 April 1973. Later it was moved to the Mid Hants Railway for full restoration. It was the second Bulleid light Pacific to leave Barry; by 2016 all but two of the twenty survivors had operated in preservation – a remarkable achievement (excluding *Winston Churchill*, a restored static exhibit).

Preston has a very impressive station and on 7 May 1973, the date of my first visit, there was plenty to see. In those pre-electrification days (although the wires are in place) expresses for Carlisle and Scotland were handled by these Class 50 engines, based on the old DP2 prototype (and originally hired by BR). Here we see No. 430 waiting to leave with the huge overall roof in the background. The head code indicates a service going through to Scotland.

In the days just before the BR diesel fleet was renumbered with TOPS identities, a Class 40 Type 4, No. 373, is seen here on 7 May 1973 at Preston station with a northbound freight. By this time, these early diesels were increasingly relegated to freight work.

Here we have the normal situation on the Midland main line in the 1970s. With a whiff of steam around the coupling, a grubby Peak Class 45 diesel, No. 77 *Royal Irish Fusilier*, is waiting at St Pancras to leave with a northbound express. The transformation of this lovely old station has been so complete that, even with the classic architecture, today it simply feels like a different place. The border round the nameplate is unusual on this class, although one or two others also had the same style. This picture was taken on 7 May 1973. Twelve years later as No. 45004 she was withdrawn. The 'St Pancras' arrow on the signal box seems rather superfluous.

Two Class 86 engines Nos E3139 and E3159, are seen in this busy 'end of platform' view at Euston on 7 May 1973. I believe E3159 is still running as 86628, so it's given very good service over the years. The Class 86 and 87 electrics held sway here for thirty years.

The peace at Bicester North station is briefly broken by the arrival of a Gloucester RCW single unit railcar heading south on 27 April 1973. The station sign merely says 'Bicester' as the old LNWR Town station was closed at this time. Photographed during its lean years, this was once a main line welcoming Kings and Castles and is now much busier again.

No. 1044 *Western Duchess* is seen here near Bicester London Road station on 27 April 1973 heading east with a stone train – either for building work at Milton Keynes or Northampton. (I think it was a bit late in the day for the Northampton train, which arrived at Castle station around noon.) These engines were by now often working freights. The line is the Oxford–Bletchley route, which has been mothballed for many years, but is now enjoying a revival.

A lovely spring day, 2 March 1973, was good for photography, so I took my camera to the Northampton–Market Harborough branch to see if anything was moving. I started at Draughton, but have now reached Spratton crossing, where we see a freshly painted Class 25 No. 7530 heading south with a mixed freight. BR tried hard to close this line but kept finding reasons to keep it open until the early 1980s, when at last it succumbed. The mixed set of wagons shows BR was still in the individual wagon load business in the early 1970s.

On 2 March 1973 a stone train arrives at Northampton station headed by Western Class diesel No. 1072 *Western Glory*. Already the short reign of these engines on express trains was virtually over and as a non-standard type their future was bleak. These stone trains were a regular occurrence, arriving from Westbury via Oxford and Bletchley and then reversing to Far Cotton sidings for unloading. It was stone for the expansion of Northampton. On this day I got a ride on the train down to Far Cotton, thanks to a friendly station manager. Just look at the sacks of mail everywhere.

A two car Metro-Cammell DMU is seen at Carnforth on 7 May 1973 with a Morecambe service. An eclectic mix of late '60s cars provides a tease for car-spotters.

Here I was at Preston and met an old friend, one of the West Coast route English Electric Type 4 engines, No. 214 *Antonia*. It is standing in the station while parcels are loaded on 7 May 1973.

An express arriving at Paddington on 8 May 1973 is headed by Class 52 diesel hydraulic No. 1044 *Western Duchess* in the period when the Westerns were being relieved of top link work by Brush Class 47 locomotives. This was probably the best of my 400 mm 'long lens' Paddington shots, which were not helped by a very gloomy morning. I came to understand that this massive lens needed lots of light. I had photographed this engine on a stone train at Bicester two weeks earlier, yet within two years it was gone.

I have now reached Birmingham New Street, having travelled behind a Class 47 from Paddington via Leamington and Coventry. Birmingham Snow Hill had been closed the previous year. One of the first trains I saw was this inter-regional service hauled by Peak No. 71 *The Staffordshire Regiment (Prince of Wales's)*, later 45049. Meanwhile a Euston train will be headed by Class 86 No. E3171, which is also moving into the station on 8 May 1973. New Street was always busy, busy.

Here is a short-lived number, 86201, on a BR electric locomotive. No. E3191 became the very first Class 86/2 engine in 1972, but was then rebuilt to Class 87 specification to become the first Class 86/1. In that form it was renumbered 86101 and named *Sir William Stanier FRS* and still survives today. This was the first Class 86 I photographed without the 'E' numbers and carrying a TOPS number instead. The engine is at Birmingham New Street on 8 May 1973.

An aggressive, smoky, northbound departure from Crewe on 8 May 1973 with two Class 50s heading for Glasgow – Nos 443 and 444. You can also see a Class 24 and a Class 40 on what was a very busy day. Use of these engines in pairs allowed acceleration of Anglo-Scottish expresses, completed by full electrification in 1974.

Arriving at Crewe with a mineral train is green-liveried Class 47 No. 1824 on 8 May 1973. Her paintwork (with no logo) looks good – many of the remaining green engines were looking very tatty by this time. She became 47343 and about twenty years later was written off after an accident.

Only three Cravens motor parcels vans were built and this one, M55997, is the first of them. She is seen here towing a couple of vans arriving at Shrewsbury on 9 May 1973, where I was changing trains to travel to Aberystwyth. These vehicles became Class 129 but were withdrawn soon after I took this picture. They illustrate that BR not only got itself into a muddle with diesel engine orders, but also with diesel multiple units, the clamour for new trains leading to orders being placed with several different companies.

Having now arrived at Aberystwyth, my DMU service is on the left, while a Class 24/2 diesel, No. 5142, in battered green livery waits to leave with a short parcels train from Aberystwyth to York This engine was a regular on the Cambrian lines at this time. It outlived most of its compatriots by becoming a train heating unit and was not cut up until the early 1980s. Here, on 9 May 1973, No. 5142 has had a temporary repair with a panel from a blue engine. It will head the train as far as Shrewsbury.

Vale of Rheidol 2-6-2T No. 7 *Owain Glyndwr*, in BR blue livery, has got the right of way and is starting away from Aberystwyth on the persistent climb up to Devil's Bridge, a great ride if you have never tried it. (9 May 1973). Opinions vary on the wisdom of painting these old-timers in rail blue – I think it looks absurd. They were BR's only steam engines by this time.

On this day I took the bus from Northampton to Kettering, ready to catch the Thames-Clyde Express to Carlisle. While waiting at Kettering, I extracted my borrowed bazooka-size telephoto lens and set it up at the north end of the station. The first train to catch my eye was this one, racing south behind Peak diesel No. 91 on 10 May 1973.

The Thames-Clyde Express has now reached Skipton, having reversed at Leeds during a lengthy stop, with Class 45 No. D87 in charge. As we passed through the station I leaned out of the window to take a picture of a smart Brush Type 2 diesel, No. 5808, which was messing around shunting wagons in the station. The gallows-like structure behind it looks ominous, and everywhere there is the sign of the old railway. 10 May 1973.

Bravely sporting a coat of jazzy blue paint is BR/Sulzer Type 2 No. 5024. There were 462 of these engines in service at the time (including the improved Class 25). This engine is seen at Manchester Victoria station on 11 May 1973; she was probably on station pilot duties, for which a whole army of locomotives was kept busy in the 1960s and '70s.

At Coventry station on the evening of 11 May 1973 it was a pleasure to see Class 40 No. 301, which had arrived with a very short parcels train. The driver looks happy to be photographed as he moves away and the engine is still in green livery. This was an old stamping ground for the class, but by this time they were becoming quite rare around here.

I made my way to the diesel servicing point at Oxford on 22 May 1973. Being maintained there was a Class 52 diesel, No. D1005 *Western Venturer*, with a Brush Type 4 behind. D1005 was eleven years old at this time, with just three more to run. Notice the weary, tired look and the broken screen wiper – an asset BR no longer cared about.

It is now 21 June 1973 and on the longest day of the year I have taken a short trip to Roade, near Northampton. Here the West Coast main line is in a deep cutting, with the Northampton line even lower beneath a canopy of reinforcing metalwork. Taking the main line direct to Rugby is Class AL6 No. E3130 with a container train, when such movements were something of a novelty. Nowadays I am sure many of us yearn for the variety of a long train of mixed four-wheel wagons. I gather this engine is still in use as 86637 with Freightliner, so it doesn't owe the railways any money! Notice the huge pantograph.

This picture was taken in the days when the new TOPS numbers (introduced eleven months earlier) were still something of a novelty. Here we see a North British Class AL4 – once E3045, but now showing its new number 84010 – as it heads a northbound freight at Ashton in Northamptonshire on 21 June 1973. Soon it will be swinging off to take the Northampton loop. These rather unsuccessful engines were built in Glasgow and I believe this one was the last survivor when withdrawn in 1980. Notice the fairly clear embankments – today the whole area is completely overgrown.

At Leeds City station on 11 May 1973 a train for Kings Cross waits to leave behind Deltic locomotive No. 9000 *Royal Scots Grey*. At this time these were the ultimate diesel express engines, but the arrival of the first HST units two years later signalled the end for these locomotives, which performed very well, but were expensive to maintain. My friend Bob Mullins, who took some of the pictures in this album, is involved with the preservation of two of these engines and the technical challenges involved in keeping them running must be daunting.

At the Great Western Centre, Didcot, two Gresley engines – *Sir Nigel Gresley* and *Green Arrow* – are serviced among huge crowds, having arrived with specials. Also seen are *Shannon* and 2-6-2T No. 6106. The 'Return to Steam' fever was in full swing and people just could not get enough steam at the time. 1 June 1973.

Heading north through Sandy station in Bedfordshire is Brush Class 47 diesel No. 1511 on 16 August 1973 – a perfect day for taking photographs. I shuttled between Hitchin and Sandy; the engine was running very fast, with Sandy's trees reflected in the paintwork. The station itself had not changed much since steam days. There was a real bottleneck here for many years, as four tracks condensed into two, but this was sorted out in the 1970s.

Another of the early Class 47/4 engines is seen here on a train from Leeds to Kings Cross. This time it is No. 1517, which is passing beneath the old bridge carrying the dismantled Sandy–Bedford line, so this is a bit of a nostalgic picture for me as I used this branch line so many times. The date is 16 August 1973 – more than forty-three years ago. Controversy still rages about the closure of the Oxford–Cambridge line and it seems likely that it will be reinstated throughout one day, which will almost certainly mean putting back the bridge you see here.

We are now at Hitchin station and a very mixed short freight from Letchworth to Welwyn Garden City is passing through southbound hauled by Brush Class 31 No. 5649 on 16 August 1973. Despite all the improvements over the past years, there was still a place for trains like this on BR in the early 1970s.

The Settle–Carlisle could often be relied upon to produce some unusual combinations, but this was the only time I saw an English Electric Type 4 piloting a Class 46. Sadly, it was a typically grey Pennine day when I arrived at Settle station on 1 November 1973 to begin a day's photography. Things brightened up when the first train arrived, however, with these two Type 4 diesels providing more than adequate motive power. The lead engine – No. 220 *Franconia* – is a refugee from the West Coast main line, while No. 165 is a Class 46 version of the Peak diesels.

This is one of my favourite diesel photographs. It shows a newly renumbered Class 25 and a Class 45 passing each other at Dent on a very autumnal 1 November 1973 and, as you might guess from the angle, I did not get the number of either locomotive.

Class 45 diesel No. 64 *Coldstream Guardsman* has reached the end of a long climb as it passes Ais Gill summit on 1 November 1973. The train is heading for Glasgow.

On 2 March 1973 a pair of Sulzer Type 2 locomotives, Nos 5250 and 5242, enter Northampton station running north 'wrong line' with a coal train; I assume the reason for this was to allow the train to work off the Roade line and then back down to Far Cotton. It will then head for Northampton power station where it will gain access by reversing again after Hardingstone Crossing. The fascinating red sign warns drivers not to take electric trains onto the up Blisworth line. Makes sense – it wasn't electrified! A pair of 25s was the usual power for these trains at this time.

I was on my way from Whitby to Middlesbrough by train – here our Metro-Cammell diesel unit (this is the rear end) waits at Battersby under a threatening sky on 13 September 1974.

What can they be thinking of? This is the only Standard Class 8P locomotive – No. 71000 *Duke of Gloucester* – and a group of indefatigable individuals is proposing to restore her. We used to see her regularly on the Mid-day Scot and after withdrawal she stood complete for around two years at Crewe North shed awaiting a call to preservation that never came. This picture shows her at Loughborough on 12 May 1974, shortly after arriving from Barry scrapyard (with, I believe, the smoke deflectors from a 9F).

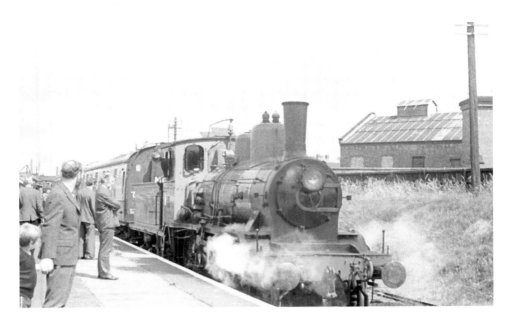

From acorns to mighty oaks... On Sunday, 14 July 1974, the 2-6-0 locomotive *King Haakon VII* is seen in action at Loughborough station during the early days of the Great Central Railway. At that time keeping a service running was a real struggle. Richard Willis and Bruce and Beryl Lovatt are the three figures in the foreground – they were the Chairman and Treasurer (and his wife) of the Main Line Steam Trust, which was the organisation that got the Great Central project under way.

My first visit to the North York Moors Railway was on 9 September 1974 and our run to Pickering was behind this slightly uninteresting but very competent 0-6-2T, No. 29. Here she is seen awaiting departure from Grosmont.

On 27 May 1975, fifteen years too late, I paid my first ever visit to the Lickey Incline. I am sorry I did not get there in steam days, but you can't do everything on 5 shillings (25p) a week pocket money! Here we see Class 46 locomotive No. 46002 climbing northwards with a Bristol to Newcastle express unassisted in pleasant sunshine and making a lot of noise. Class 37 bankers helped to give freights a shove.

I am now at Warwick station on 14 June 1975. Passing through this station is a ballast train headed by Class 25 No. 25301 and it is catching the attention of the platform-enders who had returned in some numbers in the years since steam departed.

We conclude in East Anglia. On 22 June 1975, I photographed a Metro-Cammell diesel unit arriving at Wroxham station heading for Norwich. In these days there was a junction just north of the station where trains could go either to County School or Sheringham. Now, only the Sheringham line remains, but the Bure Valley Railway uses part of the lifted County School line.

A Cravens diesel multiple unit pulling a van is approaching the swing bridge at Reedham in Norfolk on 24 June 1975. It is working a Norwich–Lowestoft service. Notice the check rails. I believe the church tower is at Halvergate. The cutting in the background was created for a long-lifted line to Yarmouth.

A Gloucester RCW two-car diesel unit is seen here in the late afternoon sunshine on its way from Haddiscoe station alongside the New Cut in Norfolk heading for Norwich. In the distance you can see in the river the remains of the swing bridge at Haddiscoe High Level, which once carried expresses from Liverpool Street to Yarmouth, together with its very prominent signal box on the right. That line was closed because of the cost of maintaining the swing bridges here and at Beccles. (25 June 1975).

Bibliography

Evans, J. *Last Rites* (Stroud, Amberley Publishing, 2016)

Haresnape, B. *British Rail Fleet Survey – Early Prototype and Pilot Scheme Diesel-Electrics* (Shepperton, Ian Allan, 1981)

Reed, B. *Diesel Hydraulic Locomotives of the Western Region* (Newton Abbot, David and Charles, 1974)

British Railways Locomotives and Other Motive Power (London, Ian Allan, 1964)

British Railways Locomotives and Other Motive Power (London, Ian Allan, 1967)

Williams, A. and Percival, D. (eds) *British Railways Locomotives and Other Motive Power* (Shepperton, Ian Allan, 1971)

Williams, A. and Percival, D. (eds) *British Railways Locomotives and Other Motive Power* (Shepperton, Ian Allan, 1973)

Williams, A. and Percival, D. (eds) *British Railways Locomotives and Other Motive Power* (Shepperton, Ian Allan, 1974)

Williams, A. and Percival, D. (eds) *British Railways Locomotives and Other Motive Power* (Shepperton, Ian Allan, 1975)

'Employment in the Railway Industry' – http://www.neighbourhood. statistics.gov.uk/HTMLDocs/dvc12/railway.html (Accessed 11 June 2016)

BBC Home '1965: Beeching plans for "bloated" railways' – http:// news.bbc.co.uk/onthisday/hi/dates/stories/february/16/ newsid_2545000/2545597.stm (Accessed 12 June 2016)

The Great Western Archive, 'Barry Scrapyard, Order of leaving' – http:// www.greatwestern.org.uk/barryno3.htm (Accessed 21 July 2016)

rail.co.uk, 'Forty Years Ago' – http://www.rail.co.uk/rail-news/2011/ forty-years-ago/ (Accessed 24 July 2016).

'Thrapston Bridge Street' – http://www.disused-stations.org.uk/t/ thrapston_bridge_street/ (Accessed 3 August 2016)

Flickr – www.flickr.com (Accessed 10 July 2016)

Shap by Peter Handford, Argo Transacord Records, DA7 (1961)

Various issues *Railway Magazine* (Tothill Press, London)

Various issues *Modern Railways* (Ian Allan, Shepperton)

Various issues *Railway World* (Ian Allan, Shepperton)

Various issues *Stephenson Locomotive Society Journal* (SLS, London)